Under the
Pic...

by Rozan...
illustrated by Tom ...

Harcourt

Orlando Boston Dallas Chicago San Diego

www.harcourtschool.com

One for you. One for me.

That's two for us.

Two for you. Two for me.

That's four for us.

Three for you. Three for me.

That's six for us.

All under the picnic tree!